PRAISE FOR FIFTY MOTHERS

"Preeti Vangani's poems are a thick braid of grief and joy, deftly weaving fifty mothers, a gone mother, a father yawning like an animal—all of that an insistent reminder that we never carry just one sorrow, never just one joy. This collection teaches us wild and unruly lessons about how love doesn't quit, even when the body does."

—AIMEE NEZHUKUMATATHIL, author of *Night Owl*

"Preeti Vangani's *Fifty Mothers* unravels and rebraids the elegy with startling tenderness and lyrical rawness: 'I rummage through the squalor of grief.' These poems are layered with invocation as each object, each relationship is placed on the altar of the poetic line. *Fifty Mothers* asks what it means to mother and to daughter, as a verb dedicated to proximity, to getting closer and closer still. Vangani's imagery is lush and bodily, simultaneously precise and bewildering: 'I have held the pink apples rolling off my mother's cheeks.' I am in awe of *Fifty Mothers* and its ever-expanding portals of grief, of love, of sensory memory."

—JANE WONG, author of *How to Not Be Afraid of Everything*

"Preeti Vangani's beautiful and poignant *Fifty Mothers* is an elegy for a mother, but also what happens before and after a mother's passing, especially how the speaker grows away, yet closer to the mother figure. Despite the elegiac subject matter, these poems are animated and spunky. 'I have a mother who . . . poured curses hot as melting iron into my original mother's ears for oversalting the potatoes. At the funeral, (she) rocked like a possessed monk reading the Bhagavad Gita over my mother's still-warm corpse. Kill me for wanting to bleach her mouth.' The speaker's perspective is vibrant so that whatever we see through the speaker's eyes is full of color and life."

—VICTORIA CHANG, author of *With My Back to the World*

"These bittersweet poems elegizing the poet's mother, gone far too young, are sharp-witted yet accessible, heart-rending, wry, and irreverent. They reveal how our deepest griefs are still tied to 'flaming hot, binding, disappearing' sparks of hope, the heart itself moving in directions that constantly surprise. Here, a young woman's hymen is like 'the slit in the pyre // through which [her] mother was set to flames,' the penetration of grief like the first act of making love. But grief is multifaceted, too, fragmentary and slippery as memory. Vangani's collection gathers together all the possible memories and dreams a child can have of a mother, and in doing so, creates a kaleidoscopic document of love and loss, change and creative transition."

—PAISLEY REKDAL, author of *West: A Translation*

FIFTY MOTHERS

FIFTY M

OTHERS

PREETI VANGANI

RIVER RIVER BOOKS  *Durham, North Carolina*

Published in the United States of America

Library of Congress Cataloging-in-Publication Data
Vangani, Preeti, 1986–
Fifty Mothers / Preeti Vangani.
ISBN-13: 979-8-9881378-9-4
Subjects: LCSH: American Poetry, Women's Poetry, Grief, Disability.
LCGFT: Poetry.
LCCN: 2025940045

Cover and interior design by Alban Fischer

RIVER RIVER BOOKS
10 Linganore Place
Durham, NC 27707

www.riverriverbooks.org

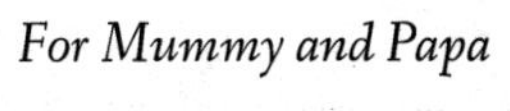

For Mummy and Papa

CONTENTS

*

Are you somewhere, alive,
somewhere alive, Mother?

AGHA SHAHID ALI

*

PERSONAL MEMORANDA

NAME POOJA K. VANGANI ~~BHAGWANTI BACHANI~~

ADDRESS ~~JEEVAN DEEP BULD FLAT 4~~

15/6, HIRA BHAVAN, R. A. K. ROAD, WADALA BOMBAY-31

TELEPHONE OFF: — RESI: —

DATE OF BIRTH 11 . 11 . 66

HEIGHT 5 . 2½ WEIGHT 49 kg.

DRIVING LICENCE NO. 83/W/19938

RADIO LICENCE NO.

BANK ACCOUNT NO. Kiran.

SAFE DEPOSIT VOULT NO.

INSURANCE POLICY NO.

First page of my mother's college diary from 1984–85. Maiden name and address scratched and replaced with married name and address in my father's hand in jest. Bank account scratched and replaced with his first name.

UNDER THE LINING IN PAPA'S CUPBOARD DRAWER HIDE BIODATAS OF POTENTIAL BRIDES

At our coffee table, I cut the tiniest hole
in the restaurant's knotted chutney packet,
hand my father the scissor to cut open
the tied bag of vadas already losing their crunch.
He motions for the metal to be put down,
then lifts it up—because we believe
that passing sharp objects by hand
leads to a fight. We share one bowl,
tear the dosa straight from the single leaf
it came wrapped in. Less mess, less dishes.
We are a ministry of less.
We are four eye bags and a race
to the remote's volume up button.
I switch the channel to comedy.
The canned laughter disturbs my father.
They think we're not smart enough to know
when to laugh, he scoffs, leaving to wash
his hands. Between our leftovers
the scissor lies split open.
Isn't Mummy smiling too big in this
funeral photo we've chosen?
Were she here, there'd be no take-out.
No shared leaf. No blades while eating.
That woman could unfasten any knot.

ASTRO MISCHIEF

Not sure what's more embarrassing, that at fourteen
I still lusted for stuffed animals or that mum's target
at the claw machine was way better than mine. Precise
as threading a needle, she'd push the steel arm straight
into the heart of the stuffed pit, wait, sipping Pepsi,
hand on hip, sure as a cowboy. Once, her single turn
brought back not one but two animals. A spotted panther
and a long-tailed squirrel. Unlike their real-life avatars,
the two never escaped my sight. Mummy was 43, 44
then gone. *God plucks some of us away randomly,*
the priest said. Her wins tucked under my arm, returning
from Astro Mischief, I trotted ahead, curious and jealous,
asked—*How is your aim so good?* She shrugged, strode
to catch up, tightening her grip around my wrist.

THE CREMATION I WASN'T ALLOWED TO ATTEND

My opened hymen, was it wider
or narrower than the slit in the pyre

through which mother was set to flames?
Penetration—my first stage of grief.

Bombay sweat soured under my bulk-
purchase thongs. The city's gutters overflowing

the way I flooded pretend moans into ears
of hungry boys. The smell of sex

leaking. Every performed orgasm
a rhythmic contraction of muscles

to forget which parts of my baby-soft mother
must have surrendered to fire first.

My earthly heat never more alive.
My body, bent and spent. My body,

a fist of her ash;
a gash from fisting.

What else
could I do but keep on disappearing?

CAMERA HEAVEN

Waiting for Mummy's funeral picture to process,
Papa said, *Towards the end all she said*
was "God." I was God, soup was God. If you
were there, you would also be God
and I wondered if in her language-
thinning head she saw us as creatures of stone
she had bowed her head in front of
or mythical beasts with wings and wish fulfilling
fables and then, there she was, out of the dark
room, developed on glossy paper.

LIFELIKE

In 1991, my mother fashioned me a robot costume for the school's fancy dress contest. Square thermocol head, thermocol torso, pliable cardboard legs—all wrapped up in silver gift-wrapping paper. Dressed in the wings, awaiting my turn, as I rehearsed my speech in my robot voice: *I am a miracle from the future,* my mother with a sewing needle kept on pricking tiny holes into my foam head, asking, *Getting enough air*?

TAKE MY HAND

A narrow lane in Matunga we would walk out and make a right the patches of wayward grass unaesthetic but lovely to feast our eyes on coming out of the dispensary where Mummy spent her last two or so months (don't have the heart to ask Papa exactly how long) it was January definitely because he'd said *9 degrees, have you ever seen Bombay go down to 9, we don't have the right blankets for that, she was shivering for nights,* and his palette was sick of eating upma for breakfast and idli for lunch from Mani's Lunch Home for forty days or more, though *Only 15 rupees a plate* and on turning right we'd arrive at the main road, four maddening lanes erupting with intimidating traffic, the road where Papa never once passed up on an opportunity to have me know, knowing I knew, *This is the widest road in all of Bombay*. Something he'd read in the Limca Book of Records. I return to the lane, horror hastening my feet. Quick, I mutter, *Think instead of the vada-pavs* I've devoured in this very lane. And three buildings down the other way was my make-out spot. Three buildings away from where Mummy died, I'd smooched, sucked, unzipped, unhooked, licked and laughed in an abandoned stairwell that seemed at the time forever under construction. Behind dusty scaffolding that seemed romantic as muslin at the time, I'd savoured a beautiful boy's sweat. We were always walking, Papa being frightened of cars (legs are safer), cigarette in one hand, the other in a permanent fold-out, ready to catch mine and I was always looking away, thinking of friends, foamy beer and believable little excuses for night-outs— my ridiculously grouchy face, as if being his daughter came with the precondition to be pissed at him, then inventing a reason to be pissed at him, and after much after, a phrase kept knocking around my head. Shall we dance. Shall We Dance. The film I'd won couple-passes for at my dance class. The screening was at the Russian Embassy Theater in Kemps' Corner. I had nobody to elope for an evening with so Mummy took me on the double decker without telling Papa how, where, how far. Because the venue was outside the radius of where he'd allow us to go. After the film, at the bus-stop, she held up her hands as if the air was her lead in ballroom dancing and blushed, *How handsome is George Clooney*. I have held the pink apples rolling off my mother's cheeks. I have inhaled the smoke of my father's loneliness marrying the eye-watering emissions of speeding lorries. It isn't even the widest road anymore.

FIFTY MOTHERS

I have fifty mothers in total. Four are my mother's real sisters, forty-five are cousins. I call them all maa-si, meaning like-mother. But when your original mother dies, likeness dies and you end up with fifty mothers.

My mother died when I was twenty-one, the age she was when she became a mother. After she died, my oldest mother's hair started falling out. My youngest mother slid into depre-ssshh. Nowadays in place of lithium she swallows TikTok videos of a godman who rides Harley Davidsons and accepts donations in crypto.

I have a mother who thanks god that her husband is hard of hearing. I have a mother who wants to be absolved by god. I have a mother who poured curses hot as melting iron into my original mother's ears for oversalting the potatoes. At the funeral, the same potty-mouthed mother rocked like a possessed saint while reading the Bhagavad Gita over my mother's still-warm corpse. Kill me for wanting to bleach her mouth. For wanting to kick her out of my country of loss.

WE REGRET THE INTERRUPTION

Can I ask Papa to stop singing "O Saathi Re" in the bathroom?
The one from Omkara: an *Othello* adaptation. The last film
they saw together in a theatre. He hums to the thrum
of the shower: *Aa chal din ko rokein, dhoop ke peeche daudein.*
Come, let's ban the day from ending, let's run after sunshine.

Never enough screen space for grief but ample
for dance and song. Can a song advance the narrative?

This is the story he tells me filled with the same daily vigour
as towel drying his back after a shower. *Omkara: a real tragedy.*
The reel was faulty, the film kept stopping. Thank god your mother
sneaked in pistachios in her dupatta. We left before it was over.

We all missed deaths. I'm reminded I landed three hours after
my mother closed her eyes. I wonder what song gripped Papa
when he decided to keep from me that Mummy was terminal.

BUSINESS SCHOOL

I've wondered what Mummy's voice sounded like—internal scream,
knife against serrated thumb, or bitten tongue, when she discovered
she was terminal. I've wondered who pioneered the hatchet of keeping
this classified. Her, Papa, or their unmelodious duet.

They way they sneakily sold my second-hand purple Zen
the week I left for business school. We are big on savings.

I've wondered what sound soothed Mummy's ears, cementing
her will to protect me from her upcoming absence—my victory yeses
in table tennis, my gratuitous yawns, or my drunken bray as *Summer of 69*
blessed the hostel halls. Those were the days I learnt

how with puffery, hyperbole, blowing up insecurities
you can sell anything: car batteries, contact lenses, gassed water.
Those were the days my father with silence, sparser calls and
strategic dilly dallying sold me a world where my mother was being saved.

EXAM FEVER

Before we knew it would become rheumatoid arthritis, my original mother tied her dupattas into sturdy double knots around my elbows and knees to block my pain. *Tighter, Mummy, tighter.* I hobbled around the house, age six through eighteen, four dupattas sashaying off my body, looking like the sickest little pirate girl. For lack of a finite disease-name, we called my multitudinal pains, exam fever. To protect me from evil forces, she tied a thick holy black thread around my neck that I'd chew down to string. Wouldn't god touch me deeper if I ate him up. So nobody could tease me for it, she rubbed god's ash under my white school blouse, tucked a smear behind my ear. When my hair fell out, a crescent of baldness blessing my crown, she pleaded Papa to find the most accurate yet kindest English words to write to the convent school principal that I be allowed to wear a single ponytail instead of the compulsory two plaits. Coconut oil, castor oil, homoeopathy, allopathy, magnet therapy, acupressure, acupuncture, prayer and rosary suffused into my scalp, finished off with kisses. Fed me curd for indigestion, pressed a pinch of ghee-soaked asafoetida into my navel on nights I winced with gas. With her pinkie, drawing figure-8's, she mixed pepper and honey into a teaspoon for my chronic sore throats. She let me lick the dribble off her finger. The last time I saw her alive, she'd forgotten who I was. If I was. *Say my name,* I sucked my teeth. Nothing. *She knows, I promise you,* Papa said. *It's just a fever.*

SOCIAL DESIRABILITY BIAS

Until her post-chemo wig arrived,
my mother peeled our every window open
no more than a finger's width. In treatment,
she liked stealing a few scarfless minutes after lunch
on the balcony, retreating when the lingering neighbour
drew open his curtains.

Those days I interned at a women's hair dye company.
Glossy swatches of hair, the whole pantone field:
cinnamons, reds, burgundies, blacks, and blondes
swished on my fingertips. Mummy never had a single grey.
I analysed why middle-aged women recorded
higher scores on Satisfaction as compared to Experience.

FRAME

They were fighting about me. Around me. A non-me. Maybe they were fighting about why she had gone over budget. He claimed she was terrible at calculating. She was. She was angry that his mother had yelled at her. But I knew they were one because they were one in being angry with me. They were fighting because I had returned at 11:47 pm. Three hours forty-seven minutes after what I god-promised. My father is excellent at calculating. He is faster than a calculator. The fight about how unsalted the dal was was really a fight about Papa thinking his brothers were not bringing in as much money as him. The fight about Mum not getting enough money from him was really about how her father was so quick to get her married off. The fight was a fight about a fight that happened before I was born—until it came back as the fight about wanting. Often it was about Mum's sister who also fought her own fight and the other two sisters who also fought the same fight. And the fourth sister who didn't have the one particular fight because she was allowed to earn. In all the houses there were husbands and sisters and monsters-in-law watching television. All had one thing in common: they fought. When the TV was on the fighting stopped so everyone could see the families on TV fighting. No series ever ended because the villain kept shifting. And when the drama was over my father went down for his smoke. He fought with god and his lungs I suppose. And my mother picked up the phone and spoke about the real fighting and the TV fighting to her sister and sister and sister and sister. Not all four sisters in one day. Otherwise that would have caused a fight about the phone bill being too high which was actually a fight about who paid the bills and whose house it was. And then they fought about how much my father smokes which was really a fight about how much he smoked but also about how much I irritated my mother about buying me a pair of jeans and a computer and a real writing table and all of that while refusing spinach. Like my mother I am terrible at calculating. Like my father I am excellent at remembering. I was so good at remembering, I learnt the answers by rote. School never ventured outside the prescribed problems in the Maths text so I vomited answers from memory. Except the answer for why they fought. Sometimes they fought in Sindhi sometimes in broken English to sound superior, sometimes without language, sometimes in round and round smoke that round and rounded the five hundred and fifty built up square feet of our two-room house. Sometimes we were the smoke of the sandal incense she lit, sometimes the smoke of his unfiltered cigarette. At night I'd lay awake in bed with my door open facing their room forcing my ears to be as open as my eyes to understand what the fighting was really about. But then I'd hear her laugh—maybe he'd cracked an adult joke and she'd say in this long stretchy way an abbreviated version of his name and then he would laugh too. And all of those nights I'd turn to the wall and wonder what the name of the boy who I'd sleep next to would be. Shorten his name. Let it grow. Blush then brush the wall as if it was his body. Give it a kiss.

SELF-TAUGHT

I wait in the balcony precariously holding my mobile phone way out into the airwaves through an iron square in the grill to catch a better signal. If I fixate over the last image of my body I sent him, this boy will magically respond. Hear the leaky pressure cooker whistle. Mum hushes it, builds it up again. A controlled storm. One semi-nude makes you prude. Too many and you're needy. Elbow rooted on the sill, a family of ants migrate onto my body, think me a path. I statue myself. My body's sculpture caption is "Teen Pregnant with Want." Am I not sexy enough to be replied to? I learnt the word *sexy* from a hit "cheap girl" song the censor board stamped as vulgar, had *sexy* replaced with a *beep*. Mimicking that red corseted starlet's moves in my petticoat, I knew I had to find a way to be sexy without ever thinking or saying I was. One night I wore a tube that sculpted my chest into two half-moons as I awkwardly stared at the neon walls of a karaoke club. I was sweat, salt, and bloody mary-ed. Across the bar, a man whose hands I memorised better than his face pulled up his fists and ran his tongue across his knuckles, grinning. What song could I request that meant *Run, but not with your feet?* How my body can be a country at war with itself but also here in the promising balcony, a bridge for beings smaller than me, soldiering to find a dot of sugar for their hunger.

FIFTY MOTHERS

I have a mother who inserts our mother tongue's vowels into English words. Pronounces *rainbow*, "ren-bow." *Sweater*, "swayter." *Latest*, "lah-test." Us fifty plus offspring laugh at her English in English; she laughs back in the mother tongue. She does not give up on English. Or laughing.

One of my mothers was born her father's colour. Charcoal-charcoal. Each morning she washed her son in goat's milk, down to his nubby testicles. I have two twin mothers who married twin brothers. At their reception, I heard the husband-brothers joke with the sister-wives, *When I blow my fuse at you, I will get away with it by telling you,"That wasn't me, that was my brother."*

My original mother was gone before I could tell her my husband calls my breasts Lisa and Rebecca. Her tumour was in her Lisa. One mother says burning a bay leaf at dawn is the easiest way to trick happiness into your nostrils. In our mother tongue is an insult that goes, *Jamande maane ghutto de haan, ta kedo na sutho the haan: Wouldn't we all be happier had your mother choked you at birth.*

PLACEBO

Grief sits in my throat as I imagine
my parents on a train back home
from an appointment with the oncologist,
(although when the patient is metastatic, the visit
should really be called "disappointment"), grief is not
that they were so easily swindled, became targets,
or their fear was preyed upon by a man who
perhaps judging by Mummy's scarved head, sold
them an untraditional powder remedy
made of herbs with twenty-four carat gold dust,
Proven to work, just mix in water, get your life
back, he whispered as the train
hiccuped; my father is not gullible but imagined
an empty bed while Mummy was already shrinking in it
so he must have relaxed his rationality and I wonder
if it was a rhyming image of her recovery he saw
in a dream—a rhythmic shimmer of leaves or scallops
of lace in her dupatta waltzing in the wind—or was it
the simple, electric restlessness of a sleepless man,
that convinced Papa to phone the crook, trade
bundled cash for a polythene packet of coarse crumbles
that a jeweller later confirmed was obviously
fake, what grief sits within me is not conjuring
the futures Papa had sketched around that
money: paint job, new tiles, mutual funds—or what
my mother dreamed up for it: a fully automatic washing
machine, a hanging macrame swing in the balcony; rather

what pinches me is that Mummy, who otherwise compounded
our kitchen's hundred spices and seeds into antidotes
for our ailments, then, stirring the spoon round and round
in the steel glass, gulped that concoction of glittering dust,
and what transpired back and forth
between her resigned chin and his optimistic gaze in that
moment—like the crackles of fire around which
they were once wedded, those momentary dots of blaze
that were suspended in celebratory air—were golden speckles
of hope's remnants: flaming hot, binding, disappearing.

CATALOGUE OF INTRUSIONS ON MY MOTHER'S BREAST(S)

The landline's receiver. And the cordless. The strapless. It's pinching underwire. Half cups and corsets. My father's head. His mouth and nicotine breath. Her hand in wonder. Black beads of her mangalsutra. A kerchief and rolled up cash in her bra's trap. Manoj Bajpai on TV. Her hand in labour. Nails carving half-moons. Pain relievers. Primrose oil. My little wailing mouth. My first hunger and her hunger to keep me full. Her fingers squeezing, praying for more. The guilt of formula. Lactation supplements. Enhancers and thinners. The nurse's push and pull. Jiggle from shimmying in the kitchen to Kajra Re. Ribbed plastic of the green hand fan, it's wee back and forth. Heat of her yoga mat. Her rosary, her rosary. Estée Lauder's Tuberose Gardenia. Cholis and kurtas. White cotton. White lace. The colours they became in the pre-wash soak. And soap. And shampoo trickle-down. My piss. My burp spit. My drool. The benign lump and biopsy's needle. Her loud, cow-like burps. And chlorine from WaterKingdom's summer holiday rivers. Bump bump from FlowRide. The thing we are forbidden to tell neighbours she has. Say, cough. Say, stubborn fever. Say nothing. Mammogram clamps and doctors' hands. A plug pulled. Logs of wood where a child of mine would've coo-ed.

GRIDLOCK

My boyfriend did not leave me because I had arthritis that would make caring for his parents difficult. That was his official reason. My body held that deficiency until he told me why, truly—I'd been with several men while he had been only with me. He couldn't understand why I'd stop at him. I loved him. I loved that he cut up tough meats on my plate into bite-sized pieces when my degenerating fingers couldn't compel a knife. I used to delay scratching down his back, a gesture that instantly made him come. His house was on Saat Rasta, seven roads radiating from a traffucked circle. The evenings I drove to him, citing overtime at home, my widower father would ask the maid to not cook dinner. Cooking dinner for one is wasteful. I sought love at the expense of my father's hunger, his shoddy supper of roadside bunmaska or anda-pav. *I am starving you to fetch you a groom, Papa, long-term gain!* I did not say. I never felt guilt, only anger at my father's unwillingness (not inability) to care for himself. To re-strike a friendship, I met my (ex)boyfriend for a late night show at the Imax dome. My phone died. The film was Life of Pi. I will resist the lush metaphors that the movie provides because this is no time for meandering by beauty. When you live on your father's clock, there is no time for meandering. I drove home to find my father had alarmed aunty-uncle-cousins to track me down. Cabbed through the city to trace my whereabouts. My father shepherd-dogging me. I shepherd-dogging boy(s) simmering their sticky outbursts. From within the cramped motor-whirring centre, arose spokes and exhaust fumes.

HOW WE GOT OUT

In the year between remission and relapse
my mother wrangled out permission for me to leave

the city for grad school. And was allowed herself
a rare solo ramble to the Taj Mahal.

Foregrounding the onion dome, she poses most ladylike
with rough spikes of hair, regrown after chemo.

A relief to see her smile without the weight
of our bags. No Papa's sweater or newspaper to stow.

No stack of snacks for my vocal hungers.
Denied a Goa trip, I once photoshopped my head

into a huddle of friends leaning against a yellow bus.
Round and round each night Mummy migrated

beads on her rosary to get away for sixty minutes
of wishing. Round and round I rotated the ring

on her pointer coaxing the planet of my childhood
to revolve faster. Stuck in the fear that her past

would also be my future—she was shipped into Mrs.
a semester short of becoming a Bachelor of Home Science.

What I admired most therefore
visiting the dead wife's crypt, was not so much

the king's generosity or the dome's pearl
majesty, its upside down reflection in the opal pool

but rather when Mummy arrived at the beginning
of her end, staring at her definite unreturn

not once did she call my hostel to say *Come back.*

MARLBORO MEN

Joined at the hip by my mother's death, Papa and I
fight to keep her alive. To become more Mummy,

I nag him about his smoking. I can still smell
the hospital's bleach where his fidgety hand steadied

her feeding tube. But I was barely there. I'll never
question if he employed all his money and mind

to save her. He'll never ask why I couldn't just leave
college for her bedside. Like an expletive held back,

a cigarette stays pressed between his lips and
he is confident that we are now one marriage

each away from happiness. I fill in shaadi profiles to find a man
least like him. He, to land a wife most like Mummy.

We lock horns hunting for midnight nibbles and he's certain
I've been sleeping around. I have been sleeping a lot

under the shroud of Mum's silk dupatta. Tonight he's a widower
with triple-X in his web cache. Tonight I am in a too-short skirt

numbed by sloppy missionary. To become more Mummy,
he buys me hot breakfast. How he clutches his breath

to balance the polythene bag of sambar, flimsy as a house of cards.
Not a drop spills. We never spill a drop of liquid

grief—except on the Sunday he yelled, *You never loved her,*
and I yelled back, *Fuck. Go fuck yourself,* my first time slinging

the f-word at him. Like a punch made of freedom
and the spirit that is perhaps still derailing my mum's soul

from reaching heaven. Instead of sorry, offers of ice cream
swirl between our barely open doors. Instead, he smokes double.

Instead, her maiden name (two syllables that could mean
She who ran or *A rebel*) I got inked on my ankle.

Slouched in figure four on the pot, that night I nursed
the tattoo's open wound with saline. Excavated from my bra,

my first ever cigarette—sweaty, limp, coping stick
stolen from his drawer. I inhaled a long inhale,

believing the longer I held, the more it would free me.
But my throat gave in. I coughed out a bitter fog

and the girl my mother once was
was at once veiled in our one smoke.

FUNERAL WHISPERS

so the cancer killed her?

no, not really, the treatment

radiation? a beam? kind of
kind of? one of a kind
she was full of light
she was depressed yes c'mon everyone is depressed
marriage can do that
or she hid a lot
in her chest no her throat
and the doctor said this is very common

among women

like you as if he knew her
her poor husband
he tried
a caring man a saintly woman your mother was what a terrible world
this was
what a terrible word this was
god works in strange ways never did she have enough

time

in time he should start looking again
who will look after you

she won't be your mother   come on

understand

it is up to you now

make her journey peaceful

if you keep crying   she'll get stuck

but look her mouth   it's still open

After You Died

To keep you loud, I stole a lipstick from your drawer
before Papa filled grocery bags with your clothes, hairpins,
undergarments, and sandals, dropped them into the sea.
After four days of mourning, Papa returned to the shop.
Each morning before leaving, he'd plug in a plastic Durga lamp
in the hall. The goddess sang the gayatri mantra on loop and lit up
through her gaudily painted body. Papa said the chant would soften your
spirit's passage. Do spirits have shit taste in vocals?
We are not supposed to keep the dead inside
but your Janis Joplin-style-prescription-glasses got left behind.
I wore them. Our house got blurry. *Can't you see,* Papa said,
how lonely I get? I couldn't say that to a man who entered
and exited me. I was entered by another and another but you got further
and further. We don't dig graves, but if we did I'd come to you,
dock a photo of a young Manoj Bajpai with his lush moustache
concealing a bit of his lip by your grass, and pray
your actor-crush makes you blush wherever you are.
Your breast MRIs were next to go, images
so large and sharp they'd cut holes through the jumbo
Shoppers' Stop bags you had stored them in. I hang
the cream cardigan you bought me in closets across continents
but fearing stains I never put it on. While men transported
you to be cremated, I was alone in the hall lighting jasmine agarbatti
at the altar and, trying to get closer, I tipped your funeral frame off the shelf.

UNREWARDING

I fish out the familiar purple tin
heavy with his old coin collection
from my father's cupboard.
Let it waterfall to form
a pyramid of silver on the bed.

Aanas, athanas, chavanis from when
a gallon of milk was a chavani. Sparkling
gold ginnis. My favorite is a one aana coin
that he, as a schoolboy, threw on the tracks
to see what a fast train does to a penny.
A blanked out metal face, a little
crimped moon. It reminds me that my father
the man who plots to leave a room
as soon as he enters it—once stood still
as a summer afternoon—back of his knees
sweating, tapping his feet at the edge
of a railway platform to observe
the workings of pressure. Just as he sat,
rocking his chair, slow as a lullaby,
in Mum's hot hospital room.
By then he was done running
her memory back by crooning the songs
she loved. By then, the only song was his
waiting and his resting heart like an empty
bucket poised to be filled.
Where does he hide his sorrow?

Between the same molars that once thickened
as honeycombs with mum's roti crumbles,
deep fried in sugar and ghee? Kutti, we call this
rich breakfast. And dad's salesman-superstition
is to absolutely eat kutti on the first
of every month. *Kutti on the tongue,*
means Lakshmi will come chhan chhan chhan.
Once, he sang for more money. Once, he sang
for more of Mummy. Now, before work,
he gulps down three Marie biscuits, a glass
of milk. Rubs his belly and says,
I am superbly full. He knows he isn't.
He knows I know he isn't. Fullness, his currency
of consolation, his way of saying, *I don't want you*
to also grieve for my hunger.

HOME SCIENCE

Mummy is helping me assemble a scrapbook
featuring two hundred women scientists.

Genius seems so damn achievable.
I haven't yet aged into bullying her

for dropping out of college. That she was
made to drop. With every degree I land

I will go on to widen
my disdain for her simpleness.

How she butchers
the word penicillin.

Pastes on the fancy paper a headshot
of Madam Curie. I will go on to learn

that success for scientists and poets
is an epiphany and success for a pupil

is perfection. Aren't I a perfect pupil? How I sicken
at the glue lines bleeding from under her work.

LIFESTYLE DISORDER

What I cannot uncork, I bite
open. A lover says *That's too much teeth.*
Examining my hips with a reflex hammer,
the rheumatologist wants to know, again,
my age. On the frown-to-smile scale
I underestimate my pain.
Five years left to birth my body into a regular
mother. Maybe six. *Hold the grocery bags*
like a baby, the hand therapist trains me.
Maybe is not an option under *Wants children*
on this dating app. I re-adjust my pictures
to crop my deformed fingers. *Plan quick,*
the doctor says. At this point I've had arthritis
longer than I have had my mother.
Dear gods of disease-modifying drugs,
take me back to citrus afternoons
when family was a game with tiny teacups,
little girls relishing sips of air, and that was enough.
What can you do with your eggs
in the meanwhile? I crack
when I'm on my knees. I creak when I say
to him, *Do what you like with me.* I fix
a strip of foam around what slips my grip—
a pen, a cup ear, a knife. Another way to heal
is to sniff the dupatta Mum used to tie around
my aching Iodex-ed elbow. To remember
its tightening knot. The lines its untying

imprinted on my skin. *You can relapse*
post pregnancy, the doctor warns. I tuck
the prescription in a book. Want to tell him
nobody is coming. Not Mother. Not motherhood.

MY GONE MOTHER SENDS HER BUCKET LIST

Instead of me spitting cherry seeds
into a steel bowl at the edge of prime time
cliffhangers, and him scramming down
to the paan-shop, sucking
abrasive puffs of Navy Cuts in
intellectual-husbands-circle-jerks,
happiness. Or is this a happy marriage—
this productive looking away?
Lonely? I am not lonely by any means
I am allowed one friend—my sister-in-law.
Our ears pierced identical by
mother-in-law cusses: *Chambo, chhori.*
To you, my paw, girl.
Such unround rotis you'll feed my boy?
For the fed boy to pet my sacrum.
1 glass of water.
1 cold coffee with vanilla ice-cream.
Do I not pepper pain with pleasure, god,
if you buy a woman into a house
allow her no trade, no friends
allot her an allowance
tighter than the sprout
of a prostitute's cleavage
how can the Great Almighty
be enough.
Not just the rosary's grip,

a budget holiday trip
a silky slip and garnet rings
and diamonds—not under the permissible
hoax of constructing a trousseau
for daughter's marriage. For me.
A paint job for the gangrene walls and nails
box-filed at the beauty parlor
1 microwave
1 ironing table (not daughter's study table doubling up)
1 dignified shelf in kitchen for my gods
not this floor-level miscellaneous drawer
(no wonder the divines aren't giving a crap about me)
1 chilled beer
1 burning touch
1 pure electric and narcotic thrill
of unstitching
my heavy heart open
to the man who snores and drools
in my armpit
without being told,
Enough
without being
told to *Stop*
behaving like such a woman

PARTY GHOST

And now? Is her celebration done? And now?

is what Mummy kept asking
on her last day, holding out for my graduation ceremony—

the robed culmination
of my "freedom years"

she'd wrestled Papa let me have.
Before every exam, rubbing warm oil

into the pain on the inside of my elbows, she'd whisper:
I don't care first or second rank—I just want you

independent. So independent
I missed her dying

and death. Where was I?
    Gobbling down

a feast of glossy noodles
numbed by Sichuan spice.

And when Mummy could no longer
uncurtain her eyes, Papa   tells me he assured her:

It is done. Done so good.

SWEEPING GESTURES

A crisp wind slipped through the straps of my pink sundress as I walked into Rothko's chapel. A dress I wore often to film festivals in Bombay, steeping my senses in back-to-back movies. I believed then that the more I saw, the more unclouded my own life would become. Now, here, I am in Houston, engulfed by Rothko's panels on a bench without backrest, his vigorous black paint, those broad sweeping gestures in a barely lit room, hearing my heart through my skin, pining for an art epiphany but really wondering if it was raining out? An on-off rain or an angry, unrelenting-rain? The kind my mother spewed over the phone each night when Papa sneaked out for a smoke, complaining to her sister about me, him, her period, the price of saffron, the thievery of mango season, and I heard by hiding the cordless in my room. She, a wall apart curling the landline's coiling cord. Even if I feverishly dreamed of escaping that house, I loved hearing her hum and haw over stories in which the three of us were inseparable. I shudder to ask my father about the moment after he scattered her last. Did he see a ripple in the riverbed? I hate to think her ash was her last remain. I am her last remain. Mother: a something I choose not to become due to autoimmune pain and the same pain here, threaded like a lattice behind my legs. But I stay on the bench thumbing its one rough groove, pining for the scent of warm coconut oil she used to bring me in a steel katori, rubbing it behind my knees with the grace of a pianist's hands. I stay a little longer, because my painter-friend had said, *If you wanna see art that is not a market, just sit there.* As I sit here tilting my head, a few people have wandered in and whisper, *But where are the paintings?* And, for today, I want this confusion to be enough. I step outside, returning to the gridlock rumblings of the city. It is raining—the skin-slapping kind, the Bombay kind, loud and gushing. I run for cover across the road to the gift shop, evading the receptionist's eye lest she asks me to buy. Instead she asks, *Were you able to reflect in there?* Mummy, why did you go?

No answers except the orchestra of rain and people buttoning dark jackets, steadying their umbrellas, flipping edges from turning. Rain-rain, dark rain. I step outside again, looking skyward to eavesdrop into the afterlife, to curl my finger around its inexhaustible cord.

IT FEELS LIKE CHEATING ON MY GONE MOTHER

driving my father to a whole other city to vet
a potential match the matchmaker found him.

My father, who thinks the kitchen is too much
of a journey to get himself water, travelling over

hundred kilometres, windows down, drumming
the dashboard, singing a 90s song in which the hero

romances a debutant half his age. Who bailed him
out of the grief prison so quick? Loneliness?

Lunchtime sadness? The lack of home-cooked meals?
Lust? But shouldn't sex have become a chore by now?

The promising partner is nothing like Mum.
It's not like she'll be your mother, Papa had consoled me

mid-song. I want to like her, her heady jasmine perfume.
Above all, I want this to end. And it does.

She's not into him, or he doesn't consider her pretty
enough. We leave. And after he too leaves me, I wonder,

how will I meet my eyes knowing
a part of me wanted, far more than love, for him to be alone.

NEAREST EXIT

Late evenings when pre-monsoon winds
wailed over the old clock tower
and branches older than myths fell
between signs of GO SLOW and HUMP
AHEAD, I left for home
from his paying-guest room,
wrinkled shirt and top-bunned, the pain
of rough sex vibrating through my legs
like a primate's call reverberating
through the woods. I drank
Merlot after Merlot at the seedy bar
next to office, salivating for a salt
brinier than the bowl of vinegar chips.
I remember thinking then, laughing
loudest at jokes, *This should be enough.*
I had friends, mum's memories,
my own TV, a boyfriend from work
who said he wanted more and more
in the context of fucking. Clouds, volatile
as coal seized the sky as we licked
each other dry, his citrusy cologne
alive for days on my watch strap.
On sills and footpaths, ant families
fortified their home. At home, I manipulated
dough, never quite as fluffy as Mum's,
gave in, ate noodles—the instant kind.
A kind of instance for breaking up

never arrived until he moved jobs and
at his farewell. He winked and said, *It's been real*
over goodbye cupcakes, blue frosting
cracking his lips. Then his desk was cleared,
papers shredded, nameplate stripped off.
Although his absence kept widening
the mouth of the absence I was trying to zip,
it didn't hurt as much if I measured all the griefs
I was hoarding on a yardstick. Why waste,
I thought, my mourning on a well-
groomed boy when I had a gone mother
to raise? If I imagined my mother with me,
the heaviness under my eyes, deep
as punts in wine bottles, loosened. A sort of
emotional hunger left my body and wafted
into the streets as the ghost of that blind mother
for whom the dutiful Jain child had built
the clocktower—the *gong gong* of the bell
was designed as a map for the wandering lady
to find her bearings and turn homeward
so she could eat before sundown.
The clock chimed.
I started wearing my hair down.

BLIND HEM

My mother's wig lived longer
than what killed her. After she died,
I fixed her false-hair onto my head
then buried my head into her cupboard
to smell her on her clothes. All I got
was naphthalene and perfect folds.
Once again, I encountered
her care before her. The woman
who snipped off the loose ends of threads
so close, the alteration never showed.

I too tried repairing myself
by sewing grief into a pattern. But grief
isn't as much a design as a seam.
It is what holds me in—
not my mother's hand slipping into mine
seconds before the traffic light turned red.

**

HOW TO START A MEMOIR

During spring break, a white boy came in my eye. I mean his semen flew into my eye.

Back home they were surprised I hadn't gotten a green card yet.

He was an investment banker and I was hungry.

To the Brazilian waxing lady I said, *Only because I am a swimmer*.

I can't even doggie paddle. Or doggie, because thank you arthritis in my knees and wrists.

Mummy was losing it, her brain, her chemo brain. The doctor said it was *simple science really,* but how terrible of her to have forgotten my name.

So, obviously, I offered up anal.

If you go to the farmer's market ten minutes before closing, everything is half-price.

A concealer, a tummy tucker, and a pair of falsies walk into a bar.

Who am I, I asked her, *Come on, say it. Tell me who I am.*

Those days I was seeing and sucking off a comic.

Say my name, I told him.

How much of my mother's sadness is her own, and how much is being manufactured by me?

This is how our world will end, I yelled at Papa picking up the chewing gum wrapper he'd flicked on the road. Mummy was comatose.

New year. My father's getting married.

I WILL BE YOUR MOTHER, HE SAID, AFTER THE FUNERAL

Since I fled home for the States he's lost mother and father.
His teeth have recessed backward into his mouth;

the dentist says due to continuous stress. I wonder
if his compromised cuspids can any longer withstand

the sugars of aam-papad: luminous amber bars
of mango leather that he'd lit up my childhood with.

Kaaka, Papa's youngest brother. Kaaka, the braver,
I'd think, the more feminine or feminine-friendlier

for his versedness in the kitchen—who roasts
papads like mothers, nude-handed on the stove—

manipulating fire without the crutch of tongs. Who ladled
Papa's second-hand anger when I decided to leave.

And I scowled—*What do measly sari-sellers know of pursuing*
art, and his nostrils had splayed, *We are land-owners, shop-owners.*

And you are us. Carbon-copy of Papa's waning virility.
(Newlywed, mummy once mistook him for papa, the scandal!)

No image I chalk can summon the devastating intricacy
with which he sketched in 2B—trees, cottages, sceneries

—my art homework to bump me from Cs to As.
Such intricate landscapes, I'd instruct him to dumb down

his artistry to preteen mediocrity. Now, tracing a hurried
goodbye at the stoop of the shop, he urges, *Send more photos*,

and I want to cement his vanishing
calcium with acrylic, resin, some grand reckoning

address. I press him to pose alongside Papa.
Capturing them, I sense, neither of us are traders

of forgiveness but for the fact that
it doesn't once occur to him to hide his gnarly teeth.

MY GONE MOTHER WANTS ME TO LOVE MYSELF, SAYS

So your oldest friend turned out
to be a Republican. Isn't it great
you two didn't fuck? No, you don't
look like a puffed up bag of chips
in that dress. Listen, a sparrow cheeps
at the kitchen window. Short buzz,
long trill. The frill of your nightie
swishing against mine at nap time.
Your skin is so oily, how's America
not fracking on your T-zone? I am
packing multani mitti in your bag,
a walnut scrub, honey with cinnamon
and have you tried praying? God
is an easy customer. I wish you said
I love you to me as you did to the boys
in college. Is this what we gave you
freedom for? HPV? Nothing apple
cider vinegar can't cure. When
your nani died, I was back to cooking
dinner the same night. Dal, chawal,
phulka, crispy aloo. The way
your Papa likes it. I liked Varun,
why did you leave him?
Are you ever happy? You'll find
a Mills and Boon in my side drawer.
Go to page 71: "Where's that unicorn

you promised me?" asks Miranda.
"Oh wait, never mind, I can feel it
in your trousers." If you don't finish
your beer, use it as hair conditioner.
If you can't find alcohol, spit
on the wound. Marriage means
sacrifice. Your father's heart attack
is not your fault and cigarettes
are healthy for bad marriages.
Take care of your teeth. I found
you. I found you on a Thursday
in the rain, water gushing in and out
of your gumboots. I held you up
by the waist and did not let go until
I lay you in the room where I sang
and waited and sang. Sorry I fell asleep.

FREEDOM MOVEMENT

My mother used to yell from the bathroom, *I just want five more minutes!*

KANDE KI KOKI, ATTEMPT #4

I don't overwork the spiced dough, flour
encroaching my nails that as a girl I double-coated

black and sucked on pen caps, pretending they were
cigarettes and I, a modern woman. *Even if allowed to work,*

you should know how to feed—how did she season
her heart to serve lessons as these, my mother, wedded

at twenty-one-and-a-half? Crop-topped and midi-skirted,
stripped by marriage into mandatory salwars and kurtas—

and every kurta, a proxy dishrag. Despite my care
to mince thin what can fleetingly wound me,
a waning crescent of chilli suddenly sugars my teeth.

Green & seedy, it tingles
and ricochets between my ears. Neither of us
were made to debut in the kitchen out of our own

physical hunger, except if you believe grief
is a growl with a belly.

FIFTY MOTHERS

I have a mother who sits in a chair with needles in her fingers and toes, one sticking out from the centre of her nape. This mother believes a shorty never a bride makes, so when I was twelve, she dragged my original mother and me to a special healer, a man who weighed over a hundred kilos. To squeeze out centimetres from girls' heads and tails, he laid them face down in his tiled hall and walked on their backs. I lay on his floor face down. His feet heavy as iron. What am I angry about? That he split open my back into weeks of pain? Or that even my original mother—who once whispered to me *I want you to study so you learn to be independent*—was so entirely hypnotised by her sister's fears?

At the funeral, one mother gossiped that the medicine my mother took to boost her natural milk was perhaps carcinogenic. Another consoled me with the velvet of her hands, *It couldn't have been that, no.* Besides, my mother quickly shifted to formula. But I couldn't not believe that my hunger was what wrung my mother out like a raisin.

In the center spread of her college diary, my original mother wrote in block letters *You must be happy with yourself.* You must be. How do we get here, to a place where happiness too is a chore?

One mother said my mother died because she faced a mirror when she slept. Meeting yourself each morning will break you, it's science. Another looked at me like don't you get it, your mother had depre-ssshhh, or root rot; the infestation that took her own mother out. The name of that infestation is not allowed outside of our throats. It hangs over our oesophagus like a BEWARE OF DOG sign.

One mother wasn't surprised at all when she was delivered the news, for she'd already dreamt my mother's dying. Another mother made herself forget what my mother owed her: sandwich money and a recipe for pista kulfi. My four mothers dressed my gone mother in a bridal maroon. They did not let me enter the room. Sometimes we love by closing a door.

IT ALMOST KILLS ME

Squeezing a nail cutter with opposable thumbs
that can no longer oppose.
Onions, tomatoes, capsicum, brinjal.
Scent of Mt. Tam brie with dried figs
on a cracker. Explosion of salt
and the fruit's good sugar.
My mother pressing god
to do his job. Clumps of her hair
coming off, which I never saw fall.
The woman in the sequined dress
on 8th and Market with her roller
backpack whispering to her good
poodle, *Ain't no one gonna touch us,*
baby. Afternoons my fingers
almost don't shake holding
the ear of a cup. That it was
Mummy who got all our passports
made. Hers will never have a stamp.
The second amendment.
This insufficient body. This body
well or not, a well of want.
The word *not* as bounty—as in
that's not nothing.
My vibrator's fastest setting.

WHAT BODIES DO

Across the nation, workers are refurbishing gardens
into makeshift crematoriums. Those who can,

score oxygen cylinders over the black market.
Between daily run and daily grief, I lower my mask

over a dead rat lying ready as a soldier by a patch
of peonies. Eyes open, fur responsive to wind.

To ease death, I'll take anything. Kneller's *Happy
Campers*, for instance, a book about an exclusive heaven

for beings who kill themselves. Or revel in the chorus
of *Maamu, you're killing us*—how we cousins, bundled

in a minivan would scream with joy getting dizzy
as our uncle rollercoaster-ed us, spinning donuts

in the parkway after late night drives.
His body found breathless within that very circle

in a shape nobody wants to remember. His steel watch,
ticking. What five floors, piling debt, and one

unfenced jump did to him. He, who religiously,
to keep the family bound, bought two dozen black-market

opening-night movie tickets. The teaser often
more promising than the film.

The will to keep running, the teaser.
I've never seen a rat with eyes more open.

QUESTIONS FOR MY BODY

After Eduardo C. Corral

How many mirrors have you frowned into

You let him in, because

Did your mother teach you to sit like this

Who started it though

How does the uterus feel under the bootheel of a congressional floor

When did you grow hair *there*

Ask your bones if they give you the permission to squat deeper today

Missy, where did we agree the leg lands in turnout

We want to present an open thigh, don't we

Don't give me Vegas, give me grace

If your fingers hurt, carry the groceries like a baby

Baby, can we be more into the sex

What are you doing in the dream where mother is alive

Salad or fries

AN APPLE A DAY

and a pear and a persimmon   a banana at six am   lately i've been eating
a ton of fruits   to accelerate my immunity   pomegranate coming loose
at its heart   bleeding the front page headline   another woman

in India raped, beaten, found   without bra/breath/uterus/belongings   fresh blood
oranges i slice   dramatic as sunsets   bitter rind on my thumb   lingers then fades
like expletives   elegized in my mouth   i am immune   every twenty minutes

a girl is raped in India   i let the statistic sticky as jack-fruit   abduct my tongue
late-show hosts   shade the body of the country into safe and unsafe   zones
and which country do i belong to   if my country begins   with my body

do i even care   8262 miles away from home   i am gently breaking open
segments of mandarins   arranging pips into smiley faces   for the girl i babysit
her ear abnormality makes her wail   at the faintest sound   of firecrackers

bursting on the other side of the water   i say *i am sorry, tonight again*
the Giants have won   the words *desensitized normal   not-news* lodged
between my enamel-losing molars   stubborn as seeds of tamarind—sour pleasure

of pulp & flesh   which damaged my voice box   at nine   i secretly bought fistfuls
with lunch money   hid from mum   as i did the story of our neighbour-bhaiyya who
begged me to show him what was under my cherry-red skirt   is stillness a kind of reacting

have i reacted enough   did i react   the night   a romcom-loving banker
Blue Moon & lime lipped   clutched my hair   at the back of a bar said
call me master   yes no   what did i feed him   i am immune and is my *yes yes yes*

a submission of presence   as in   *here, sir*   or a submission of the shame i am to feel
but cannot   or is it a tick box checked   under the pursuit of pleasure   and of course
this is not the same at all   as the news today   some say the average girl is incapable

of telling what is and what is not   rape   a pluot is a plum crossed with
an apricot   tangelo is a marriage of tangerine with pomelo
my body is the hybrid history   of my wanton desires   fucked by undefined boundaries

my ex is hashtagged a predator   my co-worker calls himself an ally   my boss circulates
a new HR policy   another girl is raped   i am immune   i carry my body
a bursting orchard   to another candle march   hold hands with women

i have nothing   and everything in common with   every *was it abuse or not* riddle
raises itself   as the disappointed eyebrow of my convent-school nun   who asked me
during my kindergarten interview   is the tomato a fruit or a vegetable

disbelief is the first song   i picked up when I learnt to unbutton   my urges
knew it as my national anthem   before they could decide   on a final name
my family christened me   Chikoo   a rough-skinned fruit

sweetness of malt   survives   only in intense warmth   it is cold   inside a body
that knows not   was taught not   to husk tyranny from touch   I forgive   me
my every unknowing   my every denial a veil for   *how could i let it happen to me*

ONE CUP OF CHAI

If I had known that the cup of chai
my mother asked me, a drifter
in the kitchen, to make her
that afternoon, which I
having blended water and milk
in such strange ratios
that when reduced and strained
the tea came up
to barely one trisection of my pinkie
(that cup was the driest well I saw,
the lowest tide) so to cover my blunder
I poured raw tap water to flood her cup
and fled her room before she could
collect her body, bring lip to saucer,
had I known that the pale, putrid mess
I presented, was after all, the only and
last cup of tea I'd ever make her
would I have suddenly been
granted the culinary wisdom to brew
instead the pot with sprigs of lemongrass,
a pod of cardamom, perhaps even
a prestigious thread of saffron
that I'd sneak from the silver hexagonal box
she kept hidden behind the airtight jars
of pricey nuts, and bring her
a creamy drink of complex caffeine, even
make some magnanimous promise

of offering her tea on tap till she lived
but knowing me, I know I'd have just
continued being the spectacular failure I was
that day, shit-talking my every inability
out of her sight, embarrassed by failure,
afraid of consequence and knowing her,
she would have creased her nose
at first, then continued to descend
on the plate with the hopeful pull
of her slurp, stubborn as she was,
not willing to peg one finite judgement
of adulation or derision—
on the cup she was served

SEYUN PATATA

Both her replaced knees were past their shelf life
yet Amma, my Papa's mother, insisted to cook

sitting on a tall wooden stool, stirring vermicelli into
sweetened milk up front, blistering spicy potatoes

on the back burner while my tomboy mother played
sous chef and if Mummy's judgement went awry

with salt or cumin, Amma's ladle, which she whisked light
as a wand in the oil's hot rivers lest cubed potatoes crack, would

become not something Amma used but with which she was armed.
This was often. And normal. Normal as Shah Rukh Khan

employing a hundred words for *love* in a song
where one would do: *pyar ishq ashnai ulfat mohabbat meet*

yaari preet junoon. So much love on TV. So much anger
inside the house: sucked, sipped, swallowed. *Spit it out,*

mothers, I wanted to yell, *look SRK's splaying his arms*
in a Jesus-wide stance, that smouldering smile, even

the sunflowers he prances around are swaying with blush.
Everyone, even Mum, locking her palm into the right angle

of Amma's elbow as she waddled off the stool,
petty-cursed Amma gone. Then she was gone—

long after Mummy though.

In my motherless Sundays, receiving Amma's
liberal portions, I could've forgiven but

the way a Hindi song starts is how it ends:
with a mukhda, meaning *face*.
My mother's silence clogs my throat.

FIFTY MOTHERS

I have a mother who wants her mother-in-law to choke on her own burps. There are not enough cuss words, another says, that are humiliating enough to puncture the stink of her sleeping husband's farts. I have a mother who wants naps, quick and mystical as time-travel.

My mother's mother died by jumping from the balcony. In my dream of mothers, a minute before my mothers' mother jumps off the balcony, five of my mothers are downstairs holding a palanquin made of their hair. When my young grandmother jumps, she trampolines back onto the balcony. She goes on to attend all the fifty mothers' weddings, where she busts out pelvic thrusts to "Dama Dam Mast Kalandar," her head lifted upward, the whole sky entering through the gaps of her slowly falling teeth. She dies instead at eighty-two or eighty-five of perfectly natural and perfectly boring causes. Aquatic lung or cardiac cacophony.

The mother who herself suffers swollen knees, will only refer to my rheumatism as That Thing in Your Fingers. *Don't put it in your marriage bio-data,* she insists, *what doesn't show won't hurt.* And what about the blooming penises I've curled my arthritic fingers around, should I mention those?

My original mother fed me paaya soup made of goat trotters to fatten my calcium. Whether with tumour or not, she smothered her rosary day and night. *Forgive god forgive,* she chanted, one thousand ninety eight times. Forgive for what, I wanted to scream. You drink eight glasses of water and eat five fruits a day while your husband smokes a pack or two, yet I've never once heard a word of forgiveness emerge from his tarred lungs.

RESIDENT ALIEN

Hiking up Hill Trail, a red-tailed hawk circles
high above us. *Looking for something dead,* B says.

Eat my soul, I scream at the bird. There are several
ways to befriend the foreign: hug the oaks, thumb the poppy,

gush over the French broom, it's 6-foot invasive naughtiness.
When you tire of what's above, look under, says our guide.

Clusters of chanterelles, milk-thistle bundles, and the rough
memory of shaving my pubes last-minute in an office loo

for a San Franciscan date who said about the fake
succulents accenting his every surface, *Isn't it better?*

Who has time for water? Would you give up your citizenship
for this—fingernail moon, owl hoots, silhouettes of pine.

After each long glide, the hawk beats her wings, restoring
her flight.

MY GONE MOTHER SEES ME IN MY GRIEF OVERALLS, SAYS

Shed the cloak of clichés
you've buried yourself under.
There are better graves to ghost.
Look, the whales are dying,
and socialism has been aborted
in an American womb, and
your father isn't your father
like he used to be—less stone, more salt.
If you must gin, give it lime
& spine, don't permit grief
to whitewash you
in the suburban gloom
I worked 24/7 to repaint.
Zipline on the rift of my unspent
anger. The unused skillet from my
trousseau shines for you, kiss
the initials engraved on its rim:
P.K.V. Could be me, could be you.
Record the seasons I couldn't:
isolation, internet, and Instagram
filters. Make me a tiger. Grow taller
than monsoon grass. I'll walk
through you and nobody will know.

SHERIDAN, WYOMING

I dressed my limbs in sheaths of sunscreen asking myself, *Is this the solitude you wanted?*

I carried an insulated pink lunch bag. Mosquitoes spat kisses on my arms and ankles.

Each night a show about two teens on the run for murder lulled me to sleep.

On my way to work, I couldn't quite see Big Horn through the haze of faraway fire.

Twice, a magpie grazed by my window.

I counted the taxidermy on the Western Saloon's walls to keep from looking at the white people looking at me—if they looked at all.

When you cut open an animal, which way do you point its gaze?

While eating a turkey sandwich with pepperjack by the creek I saw a coyote pounce upon an antelope fawn. The scene was so noiseless it could have been paradise.

I said aloud, to nobody, *I am to be married.*

ARS POETICA

You wrote in the artist statement, *chipping away*
at a linked collection about desire. But mainly you were
masturbating 2x a day and advocating for naps on your socials.
Focus grouping women about their preening habits in Mumbai.
And, in the Bay, prompting teens to spit poems against
over-surveillance. Parading as Poison Ivy for Halloween,
you asked your husband how he thought your father would take it
if you were to hypothetically come out. You thought a blindfold
would suffice to upgrade your sex life and cried at the end
of the Georgian film when the housewife secures a flat of her own.
Meanwhile, you hadn't warmed up to your stepmother, had you?
It works, you argued in workshop, *because there is distance.*
A friend-fuck who'd lost his job to #metoo hit you up
for gig ideas. *Say you haven't been fucked better,* said another.
You left his hotel room with the slightest blood, barely a scar,
waiting for the valet to bring around your car.
Of service and serviced. *This book will reclaim sex*, you wrote.

FIFTY MOTHERS

One mother said, *For your own happiness, don't keep photos of your mother around. Not even one. When will you start behaving like your feet are on this ground?* What had happened on this ground was that my own mother died of breast cancer, which could have been avoided had the male doctor not insisted *We try to preserve the woman's breast unless it absolutely needs to be dispensed with.*

I have fifty mothers in total. I have one father. He yawns a lot. Loud and good, like a sheep's bleat, a dog hurt by a drunk's tyre screech. In his yawns, I hear the female oncologist asking after my mother's relapse, *You look so well-educated sir, how did you buy into some man's spiel of vanity?*

My body is an apothecary shelved with fifty mothers' cures. But I do not know how to heal my father when he moans in sleep-talk, *I told him, I told him, cut it off, doctor. Cut it off.*

LIGHT IS A MOVING LINE

When we are already late for the film,
my father never forgets to mention
that this high-rising cineplex that flexes its arms
like a concrete eagle once used to be three
squat single-screens that shared two walls.
The triplets were called Badal, Bijli, Barkha.
Cloud, Light, Wind. As he presses the elevator's 6 button,
and it glows a weak gold from within, I cannot
not imagine him in bell bottoms and a tight shirt,
skipping shop for college, skipping college
for a Rajesh Khanna flick. He once told me
about an entire summer, when still in primary school,
constrained with limited stipend, he plotted by
the gates with his visiting cousin to buy a single
ticket. He watched the first half, sneaked out at
intermission, debriefed the plot to his cousin
who then slipped in and played back the end
of the story. I often cannot not see my father
but in halves. He, as in his entrepreneurial self,
knows why sixty-seater theatres must surrender
their piss-scented and paan-stained selves
to become a multi-levelled *home of infinite
entertainment*. This self is of the world. It has
no time or stamina for wrestling with what ceased.
This self sees yet unsees the deceased wife.
The other half, not exact, imprecise as the moon is
most of the time, it lounges in the involuntary

outcries of what we choose to remember.
Badal, Bijlee, Barkha. This self taps its foot
to that bilabial sound of b. The half in which
I think I hear him call out: *be be be.* He pushes
open the door to the film well begun, flitting down
the rows, extending his arm for me to follow
and someone is shining a torch light now, small
and with definite purpose, the light is a moving line,
someone is guiding us to our places in this new dark.

RAISING MOTHERS

This morning she unfurled into my arthritic fingers
in the form of an easy tear perforation on the milk carton.
That was a very small kind of mother. Smaller than the mother
I encountered in myself, waiving late fees working at the library
when the nursing student in finals week eating Oreos
for dinner came begging. *No fret,* I said, my register lacklustre
compared to the mother I found in the purposeful banter
the buck-toothed guy in 12B on LHR-BOM engaged me in
to distract me from pain, cramps coiling under my knees,
every nerve sharp as teeth—grinding down a prayer
for the prednisone to usher in. The pill also a mother, dissolving
my aches invisible as the grace I trace in the blanks
between my friend's fingers chopping walnuts cooking me
aji da gallina, seasoning the chicken with mother-
like accuracy, the sense of her knowing I have long been
motherless itself a mother to me. A gold Virgin Mary
on her pointer birthed rainbows in the sun-drenched
women's clinic as we waited for her to get an IUD. An option
our mothers would perhaps not approve of, and this option
too, a kind of mother. And the ghost of my own mother
my father conjures pointing to the corner table in Kailash Parbat,
a restaurant by a cowshed where they first met, sipping
filter coffee amid bovine groans, chaperones at arm's length.
And it is hard to not be amused when my father, now motherless
and wifeless, having brought doctors and priests to both women
in vain, still finds it in him to be a mother to himself—wide-
grinned, he whistles, combing his balding head before bed.

Ask him why and he'll say, *What if Julia Roberts comes*
in my dreams tonight? What is to mother if not to suspend
moonlike faith in the face of a stubborn night like the milky
plainness with which my stepmother said while shelling peas,
He hit me once, her admission making her more my mother
then I allow her to be—her, a linear erasure of my one mother,
now my mother's kin, the two sharing a skin-memory? Look,
how she pendulums her feet at the sewing machine, altering
a paisley dress for me, says, *Try it now.*

WHAT THIS ELEGY WANTS

is to never be caught alone at an Italian bakery
buying a dozen cream horns, half-confessing,
half-flirting with the uninterested cashier,
These are my mum's favorite—are not *were.*
Not the quiver in the finger over the cursor
contributing to a cancer research fund.
How much giving after all is good enough
for grief to give up? How much research?
I have seen my father research a new bride.
Secondchance and Cleanstart and well-meaning
aunts. I have seen my mother's white nightie
hang on the bathroom door like a god's robe.
Have bitterly judged the divine rogan josh
the new mother cooks against my own mother's,
frowned at the lack of fluff in her rotis,
the tiniest flaw in her chutney.
Her every sincere endearment a splinter
in my ears. Grief, you grumpy mother-in-law,
this elegy is tired of you. As in housewife-tired
as in housewife-staying-quiet-
about-abusive-husband tired, as in
if my mother were to see me, which I'm certain
she can, as I rummage through the squalor of grief—
through a portal where cream horns are unlimited
and free—she'd continue to snack unbothered
with flakes of pastry sprouting on her chin,
and say, *tch tch tchtchtch,* exhausted yet excited

as she so often was when chasing down
a cockroach scurrying around the house
with a long broom, a task both barbaric and
bewildering. How once she had the apocalypse-
surviving beast trapped in the broom's hairs,
she'd smack the jhadu over and over
against the floor and with her other hand
draw out the wiggling enemy by its antenna,
fling it right outside the window
with a *go be free*, as if that freeness were hers.

From my mother's college diary

NOTES

The line by Agha Shahid Ali that opens the book is from his poem "Lenox Hill."

Camera Heaven: The line, "you would also be God" borrows its turn and phrasing from Laura Grothaus' poem "Also Milk."

We Regret the Interruption: The poem references the song, "O Saathi Re" from the 2006 Hindi film *Omkara*. The translation of the line "Aa chal din ko rokein, dhoop ke peeche daudein" is my own.

Fifty Mothers: The poem that appears in vignettes was first drafted and published as a lyric essay, inspired by K-Ming Chang's stunning short story "Auntland," which appears in her book, *Gods of Want*.

Self-Taught: The song referred to in the poem is "Sexy sexy sexy mujhe log bolein" from the 1994 Hindi film *Khuddar*.

Nearest Exit: The poem references the Rajabai clock tower in Bombay. Its construction was partly funded by the founder of the Bombay Stock Exchange, Premchand Roychand Jain, on the condition that the tower be named after his blind mother.

ACKNOWLEDGMENTS

Thanks to the editors of the following journals in which versions of these poems have appeared, often with different titles.

Academy of American Poets' Poem-A-Day, March 5, 2024: One Cup of Chai
AGNI: Fifty Mothers
America Magazine: Raising Mothers
Beloit Poetry Journal: Seyun Patata
Cortland Review: Unrewarding
Dialogist: Sheridan, Wyoming
Gyroscope Review: We Regret the Interruption, Cremation I Wasn't Allowed to Attend
HAD: Questions For My Body
Hobart: It Almost Kills Me
Honey Literary: On Seeing How Happy Cooking Show Contestants Are
Inverse Journal: Under the Lining in Papa's Cupboard Drawer Lay Printouts of Potential Brides
Jabberwocky: It Feels Like Cheating on My Gone Mother, Social Desirability Bias
The Journal: Catalogue of Intrusions on My Mother's Breast(s)
The Margins: Marlboro Men
Poetry Northwest: After You Died
Porter House Review: Sweeping Gestures
Raising Mothers: Funeral Whispers
Red Wheelbarrow: What This Elegy Wants
Rejection Letters: Camera Heaven
Rogue Agent Journal: An Apple a Day

Room Magazine: How to Start a Memoir
Sky Island Journal: Self-Taught
The Slowdown Podcast: Placebo
SWWIM: My Gone Mother Sees Me in My Grief Overalls, Says
Trampset: Blind Hem
VIDA Review: Lifestyle Disorder

"What This Elegy Wants" received special mention from the 2023 Pushcart Prize.

I remain beyond grateful to my mother, for the short lived but exhilarating time we had each other. Thank you for showing me the stage as soon as I could form sentences. Thank you, Papa, for holding my grief, for softening. I am beyond grateful to my friend Ravikant for knowing my heart with a clarity I often cannot reach myself.

To my aunts and sisters, *Fifty Mothers* would not have been possible without your love and your stories. Thank you for remembering my mother and never ever forgetting me.

With infinite love to my teacher, D.A. Powell, thank you for giving the book its title. To my brilliant friend, Rachel Edelman without whose tending not one of these pages goes out into the world. Thank you to Maw Shein Win, Diana Arterian, Lauren Eggert-Crowe, Rosebud Ben-Oni, Lauren Carlson, for their generous editorial inputs on earlier drafts of the book. To my Tin House, Napa Valley Writers' Conference, Community of Writers cohorts with whom a significant number of these poems were composed. To Ragdale, Djerassi and Ucross foundations for offering me the gift of space, time and deliriously good food! To the San Francisco Arts Commission and YBCA for grants that advanced this book and allowed me to teach writing grief through joy. To Han

VanderHart and Amorak Huey at River River Books for championing this manuscript. Your excitement and vociferous love for this work reached me at a time when I most needed it.

Dennis, thank you for loving me and living with the vagaries of a writer. No, you may not insert all the times I am politically incorrect into your memoirs.

PREETI VANGANI is an Indian poet and writer based in San Francisco. She is the author of *Mother Tongue Apologize* (2019), winner of the RLFPA Poetry Prize. Her work has been published in *AGNI*, *The Georgia Review*, *Gulf Coast*, *Prairie Schooner* among several other places. Her debut short story won the 2021 PEN/Robert J. Dau Emerging Writers Prize. Vangani has been a resident at Ucross, Djerassi and Ragdale. She has received artist grants from San Francisco Arts Commission and YBCA through which she facilitates poetry workshops rooted in writing grief through joy. She holds an MFA in Writing from University of San Francisco.

RIVER RIVER BOOKS was founded by Amorak Huey and Han VanderHart in March 2022. Inspired by the idea that you cannot step in the same river twice, two poetry editors join together to publish (at least) two exceptional poetry titles a year, as well as the Plainwater Nonfiction Series.

POETRY CATALOG

An Eye in Each Square, Lauren Camp, 2023
Bullet Points: A Lyric, Jennifer A Sutherland, 2023
Dear Memphis, Rachel Edelman, 2024
A Geography That Does Not Hurt Us, Carla Sofia Ferreira, 2024
Pastoral, 1994, Joe Wilkins 2025
Your Mother's Bear Gun, Corrie Williamson, 2025
Field Notes, E.G. Cunningham, 2025
Encounters for the Living and the Dead, Jameela F. Dallis, 2025
Antibody, Elane Kim, 2026
House of Myth and Necessity, Jennifer A Sutherland, 2026
Scythe, Elizabeth Sylvia, 2026
Fifty Mothers, Preeti Vangani, 2026
The Visible Field, Zoë Ryder White, 2026
Snails of the Apocalypse, Martha Zweig, 2026
Turn a Girl to Salt, Janet McAdams, 2027
Little Automata of the Deciduous Forest, Mirande Bissell, 2027
Whale Garden, Carolyn Oliver, 2027

PLAINWATER NONFICTION SERIES

There Is News Along the Ohio River, Beth Gilstrap, 2026
Backyard Alchemy, J.D. Ho, 2026